The Embsay & Bolton Abbey Steam Railway

EMBSAY & BOLTON ABBEY
STEAM RAILWAY
Mike Heath

The group in this photograph from the turn of the 19th century is thought to be the Fowler family on a day out from Liverpool, the prominent lady in black at the centre being Rosa Bella Fowler. Available information indicates that the young man standing was a member of the family that founded the Fowler Engineering Company in Leeds. *S.Walker/E&BASR*

Front cover: Beatrice, hauling a Santa Special train in December 2022, approaches Holywell Halt.

First published in Great Britain in 2024
by Silver Link Books
an imprint of Mortons Books Ltd
Media Centre
Morton Way
Horncastle LN9 6JR
www.mortonsbooks.co.uk

Copyright © Silver Link Books 2024

All rights reserved. No part of this publication may be reproduced or transmitted in any form or by any means, electronic or mechanical including photocopying, recording, or any information storage retrieval system without prior permission in writing from the publisher.
ISBN 978-1-91170-430-0

The right of Mike Heath to be identified as the author of this work has been asserted in accordance with the Copyright, Designs and Patents Act 1988.

Contents

3	THE SKIPTON & ILKLEY RAILWAY
10	THE PRESERVATION SOCIETY
14	STEAM TRAINS TO BOLTON ABBEY
18	EMBSAY STATION PAST & PRESENT
20	BOLTON ABBEY STATION PAST & PRESENT
22	LOCOMOTIVES – UNDER OVERHAUL
23	LOCOMOTIVES – STORED ON-SITE AWAITING OVERHAUL
25	LOCOMOTIVES – GONE BUT NOT FORGOTTEN
26	LOCOMOTIVES – CURRENT OPERATIONAL FLEET
31	LOCOMOTIVES – RECENT 'LONG TERM' VISITORS IN SERVICE
32	VISITING TENDER LOCOMOTIVES
34	THE DIESEL FLEET
42	COACHING STOCK
44	THE STATELY TRAINS COLLECTION
47	THEMED EXPERIENCES
50	A JOURNEY ALONG THE LINE TODAY

GB Railfreight Class 66 locomotive was named *Embsay & Bolton Abbey Steam Railway* during a ceremony at Skipton station on the 24 August 2024. In front of invited guests, GBRf's Chief Executive John Smith and chairman of the Embsay & Bolton Abbey Steam Railway Trust, Dan Ferguson, unveiled the nameplate.

THE SKIPTON & ILKLEY RAILWAY

Embsay, home of the Embsay & Bolton Abbey Steam Railway, is located just outside the market town of Skipton, 'The Gateway to the Dales'. Marketed as Yorkshire's friendly line, it has one of the finest collections of ex-industrial tank locomotives and working examples operate services over a four-mile stretch of the former trackbed of the Skipton & Ilkley Railway.

The railways reached Skipton in September 1847 when the Leeds & Bradford (Shipley to Colne extension) Railway arrived from Keighley. The line to Colne was opened the following year.

Ilkley was rail connected in August 1865 when the Otley & Ilkley Joint Railway completed its connection with the Leeds & Thirsk Railway, via Otley and Arthington. When first opened Ilkley station was a terminus.

While over the years there had been many proposals to link the two towns it was not until April 1885 that a contract for the construction of the new Skipton & Ilkley Railway was awarded to a company from Bristol, Mousley & Co. and construction commenced two months later. Ilkley station was extended and altered to become a through route and intermediate stations were constructed at Addingham, Bolton Abbey and Embsay. Three years later, on the 16 May 1888, the line opened for passenger traffic between Ilkley and Bolton Abbey, Skipton being reached a few months later. Until final closure on 22 March 1965 the line not only provided a local passenger and freight service, but also became an important diversionary route while track repairs or accident blockage elsewhere were attended to.

SKIPTON STATION

The original station was opened on the 7 September 1847 by the Leeds and Bradford Extension Railway and spent one year as a terminus until the line reached Colne on 2 October 1848. It was relocated slightly north-west of its original location in 1876. Platforms 5 & 6 (inset) were added in 1888 to serve the new route to Ilkley. The station remains open for services from Leeds and onward to Carlisle via the Settle to Carlisle railway and to Lancaster and Morecambe in the west. The buildings are Grade 2 Listed.

Main Photo: Skipton Station in the 1920s. YDRMT Archive. Inset: YDRMT Archive/David & Charles

EMBSAY STATION

Right: **EMBSAY** This view, from the footbridge was taken on 18 May 1959. *YDRMT Archive/F.W. Smith*

Above: **EMBSAY** On the last day of local steam passenger workings, 3 January 1959, Stanier 2-6-2T N0. 40147 arrives at Embsay with a Leeds to Skipton, via Ilkley, train. From the 5 January 1959 all local services were taken over by Diesel Multiple Units. *YDRMT Archive/F.W. Smith*

Below: **EMBSAY** Storming through Embsay on 22 May 1961 was Jubilee Class 4-6-0 No. 45571 *South Africa* with a Blackpool to York excursion. *YDRMT Archive/F.W. Smith*

EMBSAY The 7N54 (Heysham to Tees Yard) tanker train passing through on 4 August 1964. Class 37 D6772 (37702) was in charge. *YDRMT Archive/F.W. Smith*

BOLTON ABBEY STATION

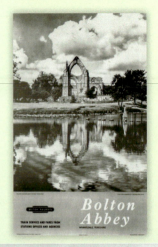

Above: **BOLTON ABBEY** station in 1964. YDRMT Archive/F.W. Smith

Right: **BOLTON ABBEY** In this 1958 photograph, Class 4 2-6-4T No. 42093 has just stopped with a Bradford Forster Square to Skipton train. Note the Porter checking tickets before passengers climb the footbridge steps. By the far bench against the main station building is the roller used to roll the stone chipping surface of the platform. YDRMT Archive/F.W. Smith

The Embsay & Bolton Abbey Steam Railway

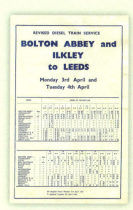

BOLTON ABBEY
Sunday 19 June 1960 and a Class 108 two-car Derby built DMU is heading back to Leeds. At that time on summer Sundays all DMU services turned back at Bolton Abbey. The main station platform once extended beyond the signal box. The rotting boards at the base clearly showing where it use to be! *YDRMT Archive/P. Sunderland – F.W. Smith Collection.*

The Embsay & Bolton Abbey Steam Railway

ADDINGHAM STATION
Opened in 1888 the station boasted 2 platforms, a signal box, goods shed, yard and a cattle dock. Today very little evidence of it exists as the area has become a residential estate. These two photographs date from 1966 just after closure. *YDRMT Archive*

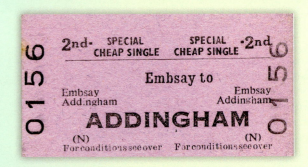

Left: **ADDINGHAM** Thought to date from circa 1954 this photograph depicts Stanier Class 3 2-6-2T No.40117 arriving at Addingham. Note the signal box, goods yard and shed behind the locomotive. *YDRMT Archive/F.W. Smith*

ILKLEY STATION

When first opened in August 1865 Ilkley station was the western terminus of the Otley & Ilkley Joint Railway. The arrival of the line from Skipton in 1888 saw the station assume the status of a junction with through platforms 3 & 4 serving the new route. Although the Skipton line closed in 1965, the tracks were only lifted in 1983 and the platforms infilled during electrification work in in the 1990s. The area becoming a car park. This photograph dates from 1966 just after closure.
YDRMT Archive

ILKLEY On leaving Ilkley the locomotives heading to Skipton passed over Brook Street Bridge. With a volcanic exhaust Patriot 4-6-0 45505 *The Royal Army Ordnance Corps* heads a returning excursion to Whaley Bridge on 15 May 1955. *YDRMT Archive/F.W. Smith*

ILKLEY With the station in the distance ex L&Y Class 2P 2-4-2T No. 10671 was captured leaving with a Leeds to Skipton, via Ilkley, working in 1948. *YDRMT Archive/F.W. Smith*

THE PRESERVATION SOCIETY

Closure of the line excluded the Skipton to Grassington and Threshfield branch and whilst track lifting soon commenced, the section between Embsay and the junction with the Grassington branch, just east of the station, was also left intact for stone traffic from the Skipton Rock Company.

In the late sixties closure of the Skipton to Grassington line was strongly rumoured. Local railway enthusiasts, encouraged by the success of the volunteers in preserving the Middleton and Keighley & Worth Valley Railways sought to save this branch line and in 1965 set up the Embsay & Grassington Railway Preservation Society to be based at Embsay.

However, soon after, British Rail revealed that far from being closed the line was to be maintained as far as Swinden Quarry at Cracoe where the works had been taken over by Tilcon Ltd. They planned to introduce a regular flow of stone trains and this mineral traffic has continued to this day.

As a result the preservationists revised their plans to the opening of a steam railway centre based around Embsay Station and the small section of track that remained. The Society changed its name to the Yorkshire Dales Railway Society (YDRS) to reflect this new proposal.

These photographs show track lifting in progress around Bolton Abbey Station. *Both YDRMT Archive/Dave Cash*

THE EARLY YEARS OF PRESERVATION

In 1970, following agreement with British Rail, the YDRS commenced the renting of Embsay Station giving them a base from which they could operate. From the beginning society members had concluded that the most economic way of running and maintaining a fleet of steam locomotives was to use former industrial types which at the time were readily available and would offer lower running costs than ex-British Railways main line locos. Notwithstanding this decision, visitors at the time would have seen 8F No. 48151 in the sidings. Now owned by West Coast Railways Carnforth, and a regular on main line steam specials, the ex-BR locomotive was stored at Embsay for five years prior to its restoration.

The first locomotive to arrive at Embsay was the oil burning Hudswell Clarke 0-4-0ST *Nellie*. Having spent much of its working life at the Esholt Sewage Works near Bradford it returned to that city in 1974 for display at its Industrial Museum.

As the number of locomotives in their fleet increased, the Society held traction engine rallies and open days that offered brake van rides to raise funds for their project. The arrival of two former electric multiple unit coaches, transferred to Yorkshire from the Altrincham Electric Railway Society, in 1972 allowed them to add proper passenger services to their money raising activities.

Above: Ex British Railways 8F No. 48151.

Below Left: 0-4-0ST *Nellie*.

Below Centre: An early traction engine rally.

Below Right: The former electric multiple unit coaches behind *Slough Estates Ltd No. 5*.

All photos: YDRMT Archive, Charles Adams

Below: The society's second locomotive was the 1925 built Avonside 0-4-0ST *Fred* seen here at Embsay working push-pull services with *Chemicals* the 1924 built Barclay 0-4-0ST *(right)*. *Chemicals* later went to work in the Shipley scrap iron works while *Fred* headed overseas to a steam centre in Belgium. YDRMT Archive/Gordon Findlay & Dave Cash

Below: The pair approach Bow Bridge Junction. *YDRMT Archive/Charles Adams*

Below: Hudswell Clarke 0-6-0ST *Slough Estates No. 5* which had arrived at Embsay in working order in 1973. A few years later it became first locomotive to be overhauled at Embsay. *YDRMT Archive/Charles Adams*

The Embsay & Bolton Abbey Steam Railway

Above: Peckett 0-4-0ST *Foleshill*, dating from 1948, on push pull duties with the Hudswell Clarke 0-6-0ST *Slough Estates No. 5*. *Foleshill* is now based at a steam museum on the island of Jersey.

The fact that the coaches were air-braked meant that they were not compatible with steam vacuum brakes necessitating a locomotive at either end of the train. Not the most economic way of running services but it enabled the society to raise revenue.

Push-pull services continued until British Railways imposed a ban on all Preservation Societies operating services on track leased from them, citing insurance problems.

A Light Railway Order would be required to allow services to resume and an application was therefore submitted. The list of works that was prepared by the Inspector was extensive and included the construction of a run-round loop at Bow Bridge Junction. Steam trains were not able to be recommence until May 1979 with the official opening of the Yorkshire Dales Railway taking place on 19 May 1979.

Above: During the British Railways ban the only steam train operation was provided by the 9½" gauge 2-4-2 locomotive *King Tut* that ran steam hauled train rides on track laid across the car park.

Above: The reopening train.

All photos: YDRMT Archive/Charles Adams

STEAM TRAINS TO BOLTON ABBEY

With the society now established at a 'reopened' Embsay station, attention turned to the disused trackbed towards Bolton Abbey. It was decided that the extension would be constructed in stages as funds and labour permitted and the society's name changed to the Embsay Steam Railway to more accurately reflect their location.

In 1982 the first mile, to a run-round loop at Skibeden was completed. Five years later trains ran on a further half mile to Holywell Halt where a new 'station' was built.

Just beyond the Halt was Holywell bridge that carried the main A59 over the railway. This was a major obstacle to further progress as the local authority, in response to concerns with the structure, had filled in the cutting and below the bridge to strengthen it. The major reinforcement works to overcome this problem included the introduction of a steel tunnel under the bridge.

The society intended the next stage to be a run-round loop at Draughton but local opposition resulted in Planning Permission being refused and the railway relocating their proposed loop to Stoneacre. This section opened in 1991.

Above: Holywell bridge in 1966, just after the line closed, before the Local Authority filled the cutting. *YDRMT Archive*

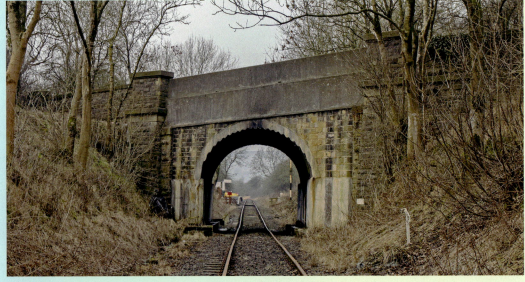

Above: The bridge today showing the tunnel lining and Holywell Halt beyond.

The Embsay & Bolton Abbey Steam Railway

Railway operations to Stoneacre were very successful and gave the impetus to the purchase of the remaining trackbed to Bolton Abbey. There then followed a period of extensive works that included the clearance of undergrowth, renewal of culverts and drains, repairs to fencing and the construction of three new bridges. The loop at Stoneacre was slightly extended, a signalbox installed and signalling altered to control what was now a passing loop. After arrival at Bolton Abbey the Embsay and Bolton Abbey Steam Railway title was adopted by the society. YDRMT *Archive/Charles Adams*

Below Right: The first works train steamed into Bolton Abbey in February 1997. YDRMT *Archive/M.G. Riley*

While the tracklaying gang made their way towards them, the team working at the site of Bolton Abbey station were also toiling away. The original building had become a derelict shell and had to be demolished. A complete rebuild was necessary and it was agreed that the basis for the design of the new building would be the original 1888 plans. However, the railway had very little money to fund the rebuild. At the time the local Yorkshire Television schedules included a programme called 'Action Time' which featured appeals for labour and materials to complete local construction projects.

The Bolton Abbey scheme was one to benefit and the programme provided huge impetus to the project and the TV exposure helped to secure more materials and sponsorship, with a local firm of architects getting involved. They drew up all the necessary plans. More offers of materials flooded in and a full electrical installation was also secured.

The construction itself was carried out under the supervision of Sir Robert McAlpine and the McAlpine building company were a 'keystone' partner sponsoring the project and providing two labourers who enormously sped up the building progress. All told there were over 170 businesses that contributed to the project between 1995 and 1997.

The opening of Bolton Abbey took place on 26 October 1997 with Sir Robert McAlpine as guest of honour. The official opening following on 1 May 1998 with Sir William McAlpine headlining the event.

Photos depicting the 'before and after' stages of the stations rebuilding. *YDRMT Archive/R. Milner & F.W. Smith*

Right: The 'big day'. *Photos YDRMT Archive/M.G. Riley*

The Embsay & Bolton Abbey Steam Railway

Whilst the station was under construction the signalling department was working on a signalbox recovered from Guiseley station where it had become redundant. The box had to be moved in two sections and was re-erected at the Embsay end of the platform.
Photos YDRMT Archive/J. Furness & F.W. Smith

The water column which now serves locomotives at Bolton Abbey came from Skipton station. Here it is in the process of being removed under the gaze of a crowd of onlookers. *YDRMT Archive/J. Furness*

After restoration at Embsay the water column has been hauled to Bolton Abbey behind *Primrose* and is about to be craned into position. *YDRMT/M. Warner.*

The station is almost ready to receive passenger trains. Track and watering services in place with final preparation work around station itself. *YDRMT Archive/M.G. Riley*

EMBSAY STATION PAST & PRESENT

This view looking east was taken on 4 August 1964. The loaded hopper wagons on the shed road were to form a special train to Carlisle that was due to depart a couple of days later on 6 August 1964. *YDRMT Archive/F.W. Smith*

The station in April 2024.

Looking east from the footbridge in 1979. *YDRMT Archive/F.W. Smith*

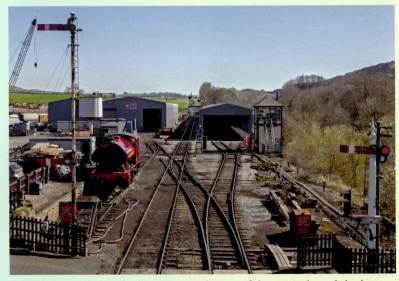

In 2023 the workshop facilities occupy the site of the original good shed to the left while the new carriage shed covers rearranged sidings on the right. The main engineering workshop building has had solar panels installed on its roof to help the railway substantially reduce electricity costs.

The Embsay & Bolton Abbey Steam Railway

Left and above: Embsay station just after closure in 1966 and again in 2022.

Right: The most notable additions to the station are these two beautifully restored buildings. The ex Midland Railway cabman's shelter was brought in from Ilkley and for a few years served as a ticket office until a former booking office from Barmouth in Wales was brought in and refurbished. The cabman's hut reverting to a waiting shelter.

BOLTON ABBEY STATION PAST & PRESENT

Above: Bolton Abbey station in the 1930s with the large iron water tower and the water columns it served visible in the background. These were removed in the 1950s. YDRMT Archive/Douglas Thompson – F.W Smith Collection

Above: This 1964 view shows the precast concrete edged platforms that replaced the original wooden structure in the late 1940s. YDRMT Archive/F.W. Smith

As there is no footbridge (currently) the comparative 2024 photograph was taken from track level a little further back to provide an overview. On the left work on completing the construction of platform 2 is well underway as is the installation of new windows and cladding to the main building on the right. The new 2023 extension to platform 1 can also be viewed.

The Embsay & Bolton Abbey Steam Railway

Over 60 years separates these two photographs of Bolton Abbey Station. Inset is Bill Smith's photograph of the station, taken in July 1962. In the intervening years the station buildings, footbridge and second platform disappeared only for the preservationists to seek to restore them. The station building came first, as previously covered. In the 2024 image, the results of more recent substantial investment are clearly evident such as new cladding and windows to the station building, an extension and new fencing to platform 1, the near completion of platform 2 and the transformation of the car park. *YDRMT, F.W. Smith/Karl Heath*

Above: Images of the continuing infrastructure developments at Bolton Abbey station. *Rob Shaw*

LOCOMOTIVES – UNDER OVERHAUL

S134 Wheldale – *Wheldale* is a standard Austerity, built in 1944 by Hunslet Engine Company, Leeds. Although it is referred to by its NCB number, S134, it became part of the Army's fleet, based at Bicester, as their No. 134. It came to the railway from NCB Wheldale Colliery, Castleford, where it had been at work until the early 1980s. *Wheldale* arrived in good mechanical condition, and the loco was returned to service for a ten year spell during which it became one of the main locomotives in the fleet. Its boiler certificate expired mid way through the 1990s.

A sad, forlorn looking *Wheldale* spent many years on display at Bolton Abbey Station supporting an appeal for restoration funds.

Following a huge fundraising effort, its restoration is now underway. (Professionals have virtually completed *Wheldale's* re-engineering while volunteers will now be restoring the cab, platework, tanks before reassembling the locomotive).

At the time of writing the restoration fund stands at circa £285,000 but with the overall cost now estimated at £300,000 (and that's using the railway's own volunteers!) there is clearly still some way to go.

Wheldale at work at Wheldale Colliery. *YDRMT Archive/John Furness*

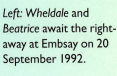

Left: Wheldale and *Beatrice* await the right-away at Embsay on 20 September 1992.

Right: On 12 September 1993 *Wheldale* made an explosive departure from Embsay. A sight all at the railway hope will be repeated soon!

LOCOMOTIVES – STORED ON-SITE AWAITING OVERHAUL

Above: **Monkton No. 1** – in the sidings at Embsay shortly after arrival on the railway. YDRMT Archive/C. Adams

Right: **Monkton No.1** – built in Leeds, by Hunslet, in 1953, this Austerity 0-6-0ST was delivered new to Monkton Colliery at Royston near Barnsley. On closure of that pit, in 1967, it moved to North Gawber Colliery, Mapplewell just north of Barnsley. It came to Embsay in 1980 and was used over the first 'Harvest of Steam' weekend. Sidelined for a number of years after initial withdrawal it wasn't until 1997 that its overhaul started. Returning to traffic in 2002 it was photographed on a freight working on 20 September 2008, before problems first noted in 2006 caused early withdrawal for another overhaul.

Slough Estates No. 5 – a 1939 built Hudswell Clarke 0-6-0ST that was destined for the Slough Trading Estate in Buckinghamshire, where it worked until the mid-1970s. It was bought and moved to Embsay in working condition (see photo on page 12). While it is currently awaiting its third overhaul these photos show it during its first overhaul and being tested on its completion when it became the first loco overhauled on the railway. YDRMT Archive/C. Adams

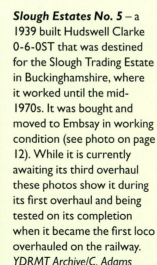

No. 140 – this PLA 0-6-0T was built by Hudswell Clarke in 1948 and initially worked at NCB Horden Colliery, County Durham. The black & white photo shows the loco at Thrislington Colliery in 1968, two years before it arrived at Embsay. On 6 October 2007 it was photographed on a vintage train. *B&W photo: YDRMT Archive*

LNER/BR Steam Crane – this steam crane is one of the older members of rolling stock based on the Embsay & Bolton Abbey having been built in 1945/6 by Cowans & Sheldon of Carlisle as one of a pair. They had been ordered by the LNER as breakdown cranes but were certainly used by BR on general engineering duties. While both cranes came to the E&BASR in 1991/2 one was no longer serviceable and resold to another railway. The one kept by the railway, LNER No. 8742 (BR No. DRC80116), is a 15-ton steam crane that was in working order right up to December 1988 so was able to be restored quickly. Since then, it has been employed on the railway for a number of jobs as can be seen from the photos. The crane now needs a boiler overhaul and an inspection of the ropes. *YDRMT Archive/Charles Adams*

The Embsay & Bolton Abbey Steam Railway

LOCOMOTIVES – GONE BUT NOT FORGOTTEN

S121 *Primrose No. 2* – this, a personal favourite of mine, was one of the earliest arrivals on the line and for many years this locomotive was one of the main engines on the railway. It had worked for the NCB at Peckfield Colliery, Micklefield having been built in Leeds by Hunslets in 1952. It was initially overhauled in the late 1980s and worked the line before a crack in the firebox saw it again withdrawn in 1999. In late 2022 *Primrose* was removed from site by its owner, pending overhaul elsewhere, with the possibility of a return to Embsay on the cards once the overhaul is complete.

Primrose at Peckfield just before leaving for Embsay. *YDRMT Archive/Charles Adams*

Left: In the late 1980s and 90s the railway held annual Bonfire Night Specials with spectacular firework displays. This was a favourite event for my then young family. *Primrose No. 2* was a regular on the after dark train services. On the 31 October 1998 it was photographed at rest during the display.

Arriving at Embsay on 21 June 1998.

LOCOMOTIVES – CURRENT OPERATIONAL FLEET

Left: **Beatrice** – this 0-6-0ST was built by Hunslet in 1945 for the Ministry of Supply and worked at the Acton Hall Colliery, Pontefract where it was named after the colliery manager's daughter. It was sold into preservation in 1976 and operating from 1982 has been on the railway for longer than her previous industrial career. *YDRMT Archive/John Furness*

Beatrice proved to be a strong and popular engine but had to be withdrawn for overhaul before the railway reached Bolton Abbey. The locomotive re-emerged from the works in 2013 and was a regular in service for the next few years. She was photographed at Embsay on 23 May 2017.

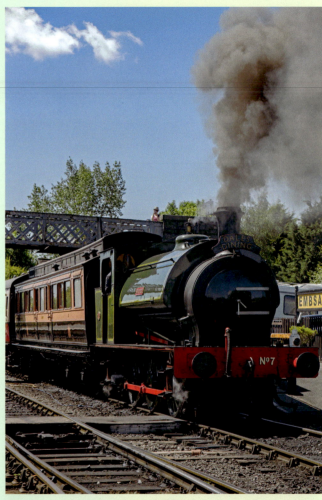

Beatrice re-entered service in 2020 following completion of a '10 yearly' overhaul and now, facing Bolton Abbey, was seen at Embsay in charge of a Dales Dining service on 10 July 2022.

Nightingale/Seacole (formerly Illingworth/ Mitchell) – this Hudswell Clarke 0-6-0ST was built in 1916 and used for war work at the Ministry of Munitions at Gretna Green. In 1922 it was relocated to work trains over the Nidd Valley Light Railway. Here it carried the name *Mitchell* but in 1930 this was changed to *Illingworth*. Following that line's closure in 1936 it was sold to Sir Robert McAlpine Ltd who gave it the name *Harold* while working on their Ebbw Vale steelworks project.

Mowlems took ownership in 1940 and the locomotive, again, took up war duties at Swynnerton and Ruddington taking the name *Swynnerton*. Before it was consigned for scrap in 1957 there was a period of work on Workington's breakwater construction and Mowlem's Braehead power station construction.

Stephen Middleton (owner of Stately Trains, which operates on the railway) was surprised to discover that a locomotive formerly of the Nidd Valley Light Railway, a line once local to him and long since closed, had survived. It was found at Great Fransham Station near Swafham in Norfolk and its purchase negotiated. Restoration over many years culminated with the locomotive tests on shuttle services in 2017 carrying the *Illingworth* name on one side and *Mitchell* on the other. It entered service in 2019.

On 22 April 2022 to mark the courage of all those in the front line tackling the Covid-19 pandemic the 1916 built *Illingworth* was renamed *Nightingale* and *Seacole* after nurses Florence Nightingale and Mary Seacole who both cared for British soldiers during the Crimean War.

Illingworth in as-found condition in Norfolk and on test in service in May 2017. *Stephen Middleton/Stately Trains*

Left: On 15 February 2022 *Illingworth* was the subject of a photo-charter during which both *Mitchell* and *Illingworth* nameplates were again worn.

Above: **No. 52322** – this former Lancashire & Yorkshire Railway 'A' Class locomotive, owned by Andy Booth, carrying British Railways plain black livery and No. 52322 has visited the line on several occasions. Emerging from the L&YR Horwich Works in 1895 this veteran locomotive worked right up to 1960 when it was withdrawn and bought by the Leonard Fairclough Civils Company and displayed in their yard in Adlington, near Chorley, for many years. It was later transferred to Steamtown, Carnforth. More recently the locomotive has been based on the East Lancashire Railway.

Right: During a photo charter on 8 September 2022, 52322 works past the former Hambleton quarry on the climb out of Bolton Abbey station.

The Embsay & Bolton Abbey Steam Railway

Cumbria – a former War Department 'Austerity' 0-6-0ST that is on long term hire to the railway from its owners, the Furness Railway Trust. Built in 1953, it spent 20 leisurely years in Army service before it was purchased by the Lakeside Railway Society in 1974 and named after the then newly named local authority. Ownership has since passed to the Furness Railway Trust and the locomotive has previously spent many years trundling along the three-and-a-half-mile Lakeside & Haverthwaite Railway. It has carried its Furness Railway red livery since 1995.

Above: At Bolton Abbey *Cumbria* awaits the dining guests on 24 March 2024.

Left: On 17 April 2022 approaching the Priors Lane over bridge.

0-6-0ST 68067 – a 2024 arrival on the Yorkshire line is Hudswell Clarke Works No. 1752 0-6-0ST 68067. This Austerity locomotive was also built for the Ministry of Defence entering service as WD75091 at the Transportation Store Depot at Marchwood in Hampshire in November 1943. Following a short loan spell with the Southern Railway at Southampton Docks, it worked at Norton Fitzarren near Taunton which was a Central Ordnance Depot used by the US Army in the period 1943-1945. It remained in War Department service, spending time in Hampshire, Berkshire and Derbyshire, until 1950 when it was bought by the National Coal Board. Initially it was based at Holly Bank Colliery, near Wolverhampton but was to work at several collieries before being moved to Bold Colliery, Lancashire, in 1978. Here it was named *Robert* and while there it famously took part in the Rocket 150 celebrations at neighbouring Rainhill. In 1982 it was sold for preservation and has since spent time at several Heritage sites including Crewe Heritage Centre, Great Central Railway, Midland Railway Centre and Llangollen Railway. The British Railways number it has been given, 68067, was carried by sister J94 class locomotive WD 71474 which was scrapped in 1971.

68067 is about to go under the footbridge on the approach to Holywell Halt on 23 April 2024.

Rocket 150, 24-26 May 1980. While still working at Bold Colliery (seen in the background) the then named *Robert* leaves the colliery sidings to take part in the cavalcade of over 40 locomotives that passed through Rainhill station as part of the celebrations of the 150th anniversary of the opening of the Liverpool and Manchester Railway.

LOCOMOTIVES – RECENT 'LONG TERM' VISITORS IN SERVICE

Above: **Welsh Guardsman** This former War Department Austerity 0-6-0ST arrived on the railway in winter 2020 and spent much of the following year in Yorkshire. Currently based on the Severn Valley Railway *Welsh Guardsman* (WD 71516) was built by Robert Stephenson & Hawthorns in 1944. After the war, in 1947, the locomotive was bought by the National Coal Board and initially worked in Northumberland before transferring to Cynheidre Colliery near Llanelli. In 1980, after spending time as a source of spares, it was saved from scrapping by the Welsh Industrial & Maritime Museum. That museum closed in 1998 and the locomotive then worked on the Gwili Railway in South Wales where it was given the name *Welsh Guardsman*. It arrived on the Severn Valley Railway on 27 February 2020.

Left: **Vulcan No. 401** A visitor spending time at Embsay in 2022 was W G Bagnall 0-6-0ST *Vulcan* No. 401. This comparatively 'young' locomotive was built in 1951 and features relatively modern technology not found on earlier engines. It was constructed for the Steel Company of Wales where it worked until replaced by diesel traction. It then spent time at Austin's Longbridge Works before being purchased for preservation by the West Somerset Railway in 1973. In 1986 ownership passed to the Stephenson Railway Museum in the North-East from whom it was hired by the E&BASR at the end of 2022.

VISITING TENDER LOCOMOTIVES

The railway have often called upon the services of tank locomotives from other preserved railways to supplement their own fleet in keeping with their policy of employing former industrial tank locomotives to operate their services. However, over the years, there have been a number of ex main line tender locomotives visiting the line for special events.

Left: The first tender-engine to haul trains on the line, in the preservation era, was former London, Midland and Scottish Class 4F No. 4422. In 1993 it visited from its then home the North Staffordshire Railway (now known as the Churnet Valley Railway). On 12 September 1993, 4422 was photographed at the head of a freight train due to depart Embsay station. Having since spent time based on the West Somerset Railway, 4422 is now back on the Churnet Valley Railway and the subject of an appeal for funds to support its overhaul.

Right: The North Eastern Railway J27 Class were designed for freight work in the North East of England. Carrying the British Railways number it was given following nationalisation of the railways in 1948, No. 65894 visited the line in 1998 and is seen hauling a train of hoppers away from Bolton Abbey on 21 June. The locomotive is owned by the North Eastern Locomotive Preservation Group (NELPG) based on the North Yorkshire Moors Railway.

The Embsay & Bolton Abbey Steam Railway

When the former Lancashire & Yorkshire Railway A Class/Class 27 No. 1300 (LMS No. 12322 – BR No. 52322) first visited the line, it carried LMS livery and the No. 12322. The photograph dates from 12 July 2014 and was taken just before the train passes beneath the Prior's Lane road bridge. *Karl Heath*

Left: A visitor from the Great Central Railway was BR Standard 2 Class 2 2-6-0 No. 78019. On 26 September 2009 it made a powerful departure from Bolton Abbey in charge of the Vintage Train comprising the Stately Trains six-wheel carriages.

Below: In 2008, in what was a coup for the railway, LNER Class D49/1 No. 246 *Morayshire* (built 1928) made its first foray outside Scotland to visit a preserved line south of the border. On 21 September it was working passenger services and was captured having just left Holywell Halt for Embsay. *Karl Heath*

Left: Great Eastern Railway Class J15 No. 65462 which dates from 1912 and is based on the North Norfolk Railway visited from mid-October until December 2005. *Daniel Ferguson*

The Embsay & Bolton Abbey Steam Railway

THE DIESEL FLEET
The railway is also home to an historic diesel fleet that includes an Electric Autocar which dates from 1903, a variety of industrial shunters and vintage mainline diesels. These see use during special events, diesel running days and Diesel Driver Experiences. They are also key support for all track maintenance works.

Below: 37294 plays to the gallery at Stoneacre on 7 May 2023.

Above: **37294 (D6994)** This class 37 was built by English Electrics at their Vulcan Foundry, Newton-le-Willows in 1965. A spell working in South Wales was followed by a period north of the border based at Inverness. Its working history also includes a year in France. It arrived on the E&BASR in 2009. On 16 June 2024 37294 waits alongside the platform at Bolton Abbey with that day's Dales Dining train.

The Embsay & Bolton Abbey Steam Railway

Above & right: **31119 & D5600 (31435)** The railway is home to two No. Class 31s, built at Brush Traction in Loughborough. 31119 dates from 1959 and arrived at Embsay in 2006. D5600 was a 1960 product that arrived in 2007. The following year the pair were inseparable at the diesel event on 20 July. Currently D5600 is undergoing a bodywork and cab overhaul whilst 31119 has had to be put into medium term storage.

Right: **Class 47 D1524 (47005)** was also built by Brush Traction in Loughborough in 1963. Its working life was spent at many depots across the country. In June 2006 it was privately purchased for preservation at the E&BASR. The photograph of D1524 on a demonstration freight working was taken on 21 September 2008. This locomotive is not operational at present and is stored on site.

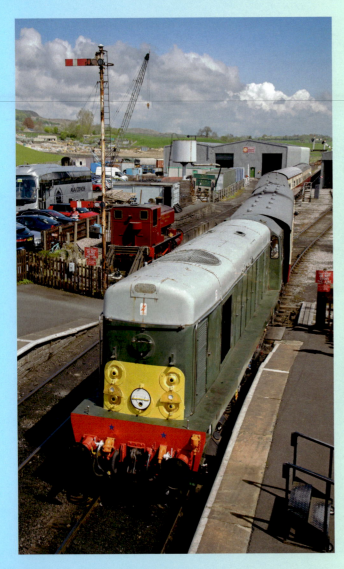

Left: **D8110/20 110** This Class 20 is one of the latest additions to the fleet. Built in English Electric's Robert Stephenson Hawthorn factory at Darlington in 1962, D8110 was allocated to Eastfield depot in Glasgow from where it worked on the West Highland line. It only returned south in 1986 and was retired by BR in 1990. It was bought by the South Devon Diesel Traction Group and was a regular performer on the South Devon Railway. It was purchased by the E&BASR and arrived on the line in February 2023.

Above: Also in 2023 a second Class 20 arrived on the line. This English Electric Type 1 (later Class 20) diesel locomotive No D8169 (later No 20169) was built at English Electric's Vulcan Foundry and entered service on 25 October 1966, spending time in the Nottingham division. It was withdrawn on 7 December 2001, and has not yet run in preservation. Since withdrawal, after spending time at Kirkby Stephen East and at the Wensleydale Railway it was moved into storage at the Sidings Industrial Estate, Tebay, until June 2023. It is owned by Graham Harris, (who also owns resident class 37, 37 294) and was moved to Embsay in June 2023 in a storage agreement, whereby in due course it is hoped restoration work will also be undertaken. *Matt Anderson*

Left: Hudswell Clarke *Mersey Docks & Harbour Board (MDHB) No.36* was built in 1958 and prior to its arrival at Embsay worked at British Steel Orb Steelworks, Newport, Gwent. Like the Class 37 it was also busy during the 'closed' season in early 2023 on works trains. *Stephen Plume*

Above: **Fowler H.W. Robinson** Built in 1946, this Fowler locomotive was delivered to Midland Tar Distillers, Olbury where it worked until 1971. It was then transferred to the Midland Yorkshire Tar Distillers, Croda Hydrocarbons, Rotherham. *YDRMT Charles Adams*

Left: **Meaford No.1** This is a Barclay 0-4-0 diesel hydraulic shunter, which was donated to the railway by National Power, with some help from the Foxfield Railway. It was built at Barclay's Kilmarnock's Works in 1957/8, supplied as No.1 (of 4) to High Marham Power Station near Newark. In 1969 Nos. 1, 3 and 4 were transferred to Meaford Power Station near Stone. Only two, Nos. 1 and 4, survived into preservation. Mechanically the locomotive was in excellent condition upon arrival and has since fulfilled the need for a heavy shunter to move dead locomotives around at Embsay. Currently it is in working order and has recently received some cosmetic work. *Rob Shaw*

Left: The Class 08 was the standard British railways general purpose diesel shunter and the railway is host to two examples. 08 054 was built in 1953 and delivered to Woodford Halse Depot. It was withdrawn from Gateshead at the end of 1980 and worked at the Swinden Limeworks until the works owners, Tarmac, donated it to the railway in 2008.

Above: **08 773** dates from 1960 and worked in BR service right up to 2001. It arrived at the Yorkshire line in July 2001.

Left: **D2084** was built at BR Doncaster Works in 1959, one of over 200 Class 03 diesel-mechanical shunting locomotives built for British Railways. Since retiring from British Rail it was preserved spending time on the Lincolnshire Wolds Railway and the West Coast Railway Company base at Carnforth. The locomotive arrived on the railway on long term hire in April 2024.

The Embsay & Bolton Abbey Steam Railway

Left: **03 078** To bolster the working steam and diesel fleets for the 2022 season, this Class 03 was hired from the North Tyneside Steam Railway and arrived in May of that year. *Will Smith*

Right: On 4 September 2022 03 078 was working a demonstration tanker train and photographed on the approach to Holywell Halt. *Karl Heath*

Autocar 3170 & Trailer 3453 The Autocar, that dates from 1903, is one of the most historically important items of rolling stock in the country and when built was well ahead of its time. This true pioneer, described as the grandfather of all modern trains, was the first railcar in the world to use internal combustion to drive a generator that in turn powered electric traction motors. It was rescued from a North Yorkshire farmer's field by Stephen Middleton (Stately Trains) who helped form the 1903 Electric Autocar Trust which (with the help of the Heritage Lottery Fund) carried out the remarkable restoration work that can be seen today. Its working life was spent in Yorkshire and the North-East between 1903 and 1931.

The Autocar entered service in 2019. The photographs are of the pair at Embsay Station for the launch of the 'Trailer' on 25 May 2024.

The Embsay & Bolton Abbey Steam Railway

Left & above: On 12 September 2020, with its trailer still under restoration, the Autocar was in service during the railway's 1940s weekend.

Left & below: NER Autocar Trailer No.3453 was built in York in 1904 and converted to a 'driving-trailer' composite autocoach two years later. The trailer's handsome NER Crimson Lake livery and meticulous lining stand in the sunshine and its plush compartments offer a glimpse into what was once the cutting edge of our country's railway past.

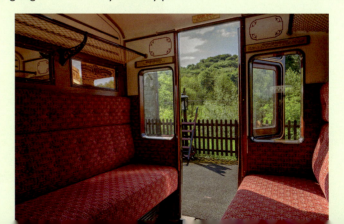

COACHING STOCK

The railway has a variety of carriages in regular use. Their main stock consists of British Railways Mark 1 coaches built in the 1950s and 1960s. Over the last few years the railway's Carriage & Wagon department have worked tirelessly to restore these steel bodied vehicles to produce stunning rakes of carriages in two original British Railway's liveries. These are Maroon and Crimson Lake and Cream ('Blood & Custard').

These photographs record the progress of restoration on just one coach – YDR No.8. Extensive structural repairs had to be carried out, particularly to the end panels where water ingress had corroded much of the internal framework. The works also included increasing the width of one door opening to allow the addition of a half-leaf to create free access for wheelchair users. *Rob Shaw/Author*

The Embsay & Bolton Abbey Steam Railway

Above: The high standard of finish in the restored carriages.

Left: On 4 April 2023 *Cumbria* departs Bolton Abbey with a resplendent mixed rake of six restored carriages.

THE STATELY TRAINS COLLECTION

The railway often uses the Edwardian and Victorian wooded bodied carriages that belong to the Stately Trains fleet, owned by Stephen Middleton. These carriages are in service on Vintage Train days and during some special events.

THE SIX-WHEELERS

Above: **Great Eastern Railway No.14** – This carriage was built by the Great Eastern Railway in 1889, and hauled VIPs over the GER. It survived as a passenger coach, and also ran on Sir William McAlpine's private railway, before being fully restored as part of the Stately Trains fleet.

Above: **Great Eastern Railway No.37** – This was also built as a saloon by the GER in 1897, and is reputed to have been the private saloon of Princess Alice, as it has several interior features (discovered during restoration) that a third class saloon would not feature.

Above: **Great North of Scotland Railway No. 34** – Great North of Scotland Railway No. 34 was built in 1896 for use in Scotland. Although it underwent several major rebuilds during its life, it has been restored to being a 1st/3rd six-wheeled carriage, and impressive it most certainly is! It is also thought to be the only Scottish coach operating in England.

Above: **Great Eastern Railway No.8** – Built as a private saloon in 1877, one of the first six-wheel coaches built by the Great Eastern Railway. In 1881 it was converted for the exclusive use of Edward, Prince of Wales and remained for his personal use until 1892 when a new bogie carriage was built for him and No 8 reverted to being a private family saloon.

THE SALOONS

Frequently you will find one, or both, of the Stately Trains bogie saloons attached to a rake of Mark 1 carriages.

London & South Western Railway First Open Royal Saloon No.17 built for Queen Victoria in 1887. Its restoration was filmed by Channel 4 and was the subject of one episode of their five-part documentary series that put into sharp focus the craftsman's art of vintage carriage restoration. Passengers can enjoy a lovely cream tea in plush surroundings that are fit for a Queen.

London & North Western Directors Saloon No.5318 Built in 1913 for the Directors of the London & North Western Railway and as such was lavishly finished. This saloon offers superior all-round views, and for half of the trip you will be next to the steam engine – you'll be able to hear it working hard and almost feel the steam engine at the head of the train! A truly memorable experience!

The Embsay & Bolton Abbey Steam Railway

Above: With their newly restored/refurbished carriages the railway have expanded their dining experiences to make your visit to Embsay & Bolton Abbey Steam Railway even more special. They now offer a full programme of events: Fish & Chip Specials, The Curry Express, Afternoon Teas, Cream Teas, Wine & Cheese tasting, Winter Warmers, Ploughman's Lunches, Themed Murder Mystery trains, Gin tasting, Faulty Towers (The Dining Experience) and the Breakfast train! *Kim Coole*

Left: As previously mentioned, saloons from the Stately Trains fleet are often added to the main service trains, offering cream teas to be enjoyed whilst taking in the panoramic views on the journey. Here, during a 1940s Weekend, an appropriately dressed couple were doing just that in the London & North Western Directors Saloon No.5318.

Left and right: For a truly luxurious experience you cannot beat a cream tea in the opulent surroundings of the Queen Victoria coach. On the day of the late Queen Elizabeth II's Platinum Jubilee the carriage, and passengers were decked out accordingly.
Author/Rodney Towers

The Embsay & Bolton Abbey Steam Railway 47

THEMED EXPERIENCES

In conjunction with Theatrical Event Management companies, the railway hosts many themed dining events such as –

The Euro Villain Song Contest. This Dining Murder Mystery was held on the weekend of the 2024 Eurovision Song Contest, with diners enjoying music and mystery throughout their journey. Many passengers adding to the fun, turning up suitably attired!

A Taste of Faulty Towers. Passengers become part of the action on this dining train as Basil, Sybil and Manuel greet them on the platform then serve up mayhem on a moving steam train alongside a three-course meal and two hours of laughter.

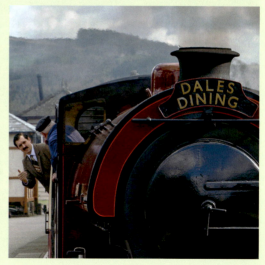

1940s WEEKEND

For many years this was an annual event where the railway stepped back to the difficult times of 1942-43 wartime Britain. Over both days, the stations are set back in time and various re-enactment societies attend the railway. Visitors are encouraged to watch out for the Home Guard, soldiers and airmen returning home on leave, the long-suffering civilians and of course the spivs! There are also displays of military vehicles at each station.

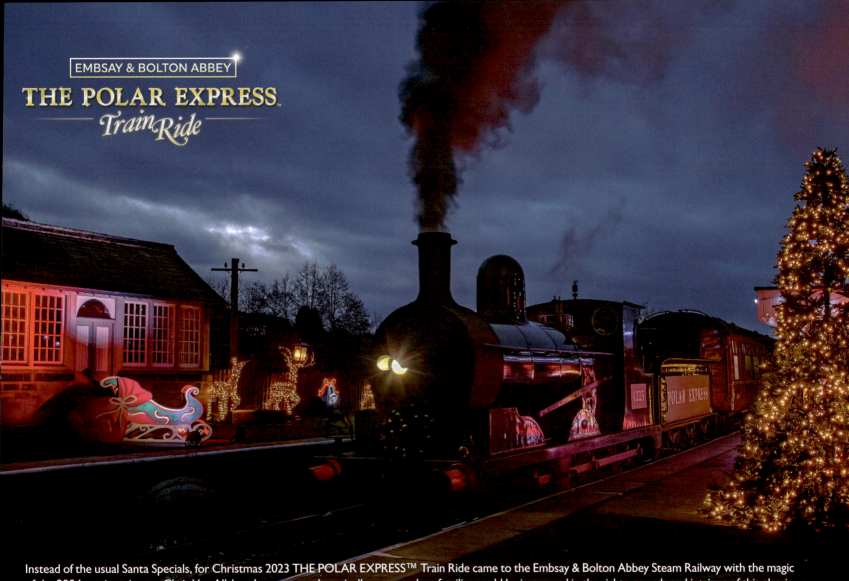

Instead of the usual Santa Specials, for Christmas 2023 THE POLAR EXPRESS™ Train Ride came to the Embsay & Bolton Abbey Steam Railway with the magic of the 2004 motion picture. Chris Van Allsburg's story was theatrically recreated, so families could be immersed in the sights, sounds and intrigue of this classic children's tale and be surrounded by the magic and wonder of the Christmas season! Embsay station took on the guise of 'The North Pole' for the festivities.

A JOURNEY ALONG THE LINE TODAY

With the rolling hills and drystone walls of the Yorkshire Dales all around, 0-6-0ST 68067, with a Bolton Abbey-bound demonstration freight train, has just left the passing loop at Stoneacre. *Karl Heath*

The Embsay & Bolton Abbey Steam Railway

BOLTON ABBEY STATION is sited in one of the most beautiful parts of Yorkshire and the railway's volunteers have lovingly recreated it in the original Midland Railway style of the 1800s. The main platform and the station buildings were reopened in 1998, and recently a former Midland Railway signal box has been purchased and placed in the location of the original, at the east end of platform 1. Opposite platform 1 the next phase of development, the reinstatement of platforms 2 and 3, is well under way. Eventually there will be additional station buildings and a footbridge to connect the platforms.

In 2024 the railway secured a grant from the AIA to help restore the former Marple footbridge and install it at the station. *R. Shaw*

Left: **BOLTON ABBEY** In June 2021 the railway held a 'Railway Rally' event which included a number of visiting locomotives. One was the London, **Brighton & South Coast Railway No. 78** *Knowle* which was built in 1880 at the LB&SCR Brighton works. Over its working life this locomotive has sported no fewer than seven different identities, including IoW W14 *Bembridge* and SR 2678. On 25 June the crew are heading back to the footplate to prepare for departure.

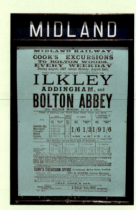

Above: **BOLTON ABBEY** The locomotive crew at rest between trains.

Above: **BOLTON ABBEY** On 11 May 2024 *Illingworth* departs Bolton Abbey with a Vintage Train.

The Embsay & Bolton Abbey Steam Railway

Right: **BOLTON ABBEY** During special event weekends the railway runs demonstration freight trains. At the 2015 Branch Line Gala visiting NCB Backworth No. 47 *Moorbarrow* passes Bolton Abbey's signal box as it heads away from the station with a demonstration works train.

Below: **BOLTON ABBEY** On a glorious 24 March 2004 *Illingworth*, carrying *Sir Robert McAlpine No. 88* nameplates, departs with a Vintage Train that includes three Stately Trains six-wheelers behind Queen Victoria's Saloon.

Photocharters offer unique opportunities for photographers and videographers to capture scenes from lineside locations not generally available to the public. The E&BASR in conjunction with a number of official charter organisers regularly hold these supervised events.

One such location is just outside Bolton Abbey station limits as the line passes through a stone wall lined section alongside the former Hambleton Quarry.

Left: **HAMBLETON QUARRY**
Lancashire & Yorkshire 'A' Class 52322 with a 'works' train. (8 September 2022)

Above: **HAMBLETON QUARRY**
LB&SCR No. 2678 *Knowle* with three of the Stately Trains six-wheeled vintage carriages. (28 June 2021)

The Embsay & Bolton Abbey Steam Railway

Above: **DRAUGHTON** The Dales in all its autumnal splendour. This November 2013 photograph was taken from the edge of the village of Draughton and shows the train emerging from the woods that surround Hambleton Quarry. *Karl Heath*

Right: **DRAUGHTON** Another 'Railway Rally' visitor on a photo charter train. Lucie is a type IV vertical-boiled locomotive built by John Cockerill in 1890 that had recently been restored by owner by Paul 'Piglet' Middleton of the North Yorkshire Moors Railway. The E&BASR were pleased to host the locomotive for its first trip away from the Moors since its recent award-winning restoration. (2 September 2021)

DRAUGHTON An idyllic Yorkshire Dales scene as L&YR 52322 passes with five carmine and cream liveried carriages on the approach to the Priors Lane road bridge.

The Embsay & Bolton Abbey Steam Railway

Above: **PRIORS LANE** Heading towards Embsay, *Cumbria* is about to pass under the bridge on 17 April 2022.

Above right: **PRIORS LANE** *Gas Works No. 2.* This locomotive is an 0-4-0ST that was built in 1911 by R&W Hawthorn, Leslie & Co Ltd at their Forth Banks Works in Newcastle upon Tyne. The engine was delivered to Keighley Corporation Gas Dept, Keighley Gas Works, West Riding of Yorkshire, where it was numbered 2. The three-week visit around the Railway Rally in 2021 saw it working in Yorkshire for the first time in over 80 years. It is usually based at the Tanfield Railway in the North East. Facing Bolton Abbey, the locomotive is seen on the approach to Priors Lane on 12 June.

Right: Creating a timeless scene on 21 February 2024, 52322 and a 'works train' heading to Bolton Abbey.

STONEACRE LOOP *Beatrice* approaches the passing loop at Stoneacre with a Dales Dining train on 21 June 2021.

STONEACRE PASSING LOOP Former L&YR 'A' Class 52322 passing the signals and 'box at Draughton during a photo charter in September 2022.

Above: **STONEACRE LOOP** Great Western Railway No. 5643 climbing away from the loop enroute to Embsay. (GWR 0-6-2T No. 5643 is a roving ambassador for the Furness Railway Trust and has in the past spent some time on the E&BASR, finally departing in 2019. Its current base is the Ribble Steam Railway at Preston).

Below: **STONEACRE LOOP** *Illingworth* with a Vintage Train.

The Embsay & Bolton Abbey Steam Railway

WINTER IN THE DALES December 2010 saw much snowfall and another 'visitor' was on Santa Special duty that day in a winter wonderland landscape. *Darfield* is another product of the Hunslet Engine Company in Leeds from where it emerged in 1953. It is named after the colliery at which it worked. In preservation Embsay was its home from 1975 until it was transferred to the Llangollen Railway in 1988. It returned to Yorkshire as a visitor in June 2008 and saw regular service until it headed back to Wales after the 2010 Christmas services. It has since moved to the Chasewater Railway and currently carries the name *Holly Bank No. 3*.

STONEACRE LOOP On a clear December 2022 day in the Dales, *Cumbria* continues its journey, Embsay bound.

The Embsay & Bolton Abbey Steam Railway

Left: **STONEACRE LOOP** On an otherwise dull 2 October 2022 a brief shaft of sunlight illuminated the very last train of the day as it pulled away from the loop. 52322 was piloting a more recent visitor to the line in the form of W G Bagnall Works No. 2994 0-6-0ST *Vulcan* No. 401.

Below: **BRIDGE 34** *Vulcan 401* – this powerful locomotive is about to pass under Bridge 34 on the approach to Holywell Halt. Note the Stately Trains vintage saloons at either end of the train.

Right: **BRIDGE 34** is a farmer's access used by just sheep and cattle but was in need of substantial repairs when the society took over, which is why the bridge parapets are now in a red brick. Visiting 0-6-0ST Austerity *Norman* which dates from 1943 and is owned by Southern Locomotives Ltd, powers beneath the bridge on the climb away from Draughton. (18 April 2017)

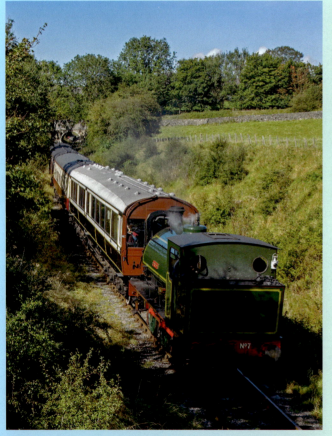

Left: **BRIDGE 34** *Beatrice* is approaching the bridge from the 'Embsay' side. The A59 bridge can just be seen above the last carriage.

Right: **HOLYWELL HALT** Before arriving at Holywell Halt the train has to pass beneath the bridge that carries the busy A59 road over the line. The concrete surrounded Armco arch, inserted to strengthen the structure can clearly be determined in this shot of the approaching Autocar.

HOLYWELL HALT *Cumbria* approaches the A59 bridge on the 18 April 2023.

The Embsay & Bolton Abbey Steam Railway

HOLYWELL HALT
The new Halt was built by volunteers and named after an old well. The cutting by the bridge is designated a 'Site of Scientific Interest' as there is visible evidence of the South Craven Fault in the rocky outcrop.

Above: **HOLYWELL HALT** *Lucie* starred at the 1940s Weekend in 2021 and looks the part on the Vintage Train.

Right: **HOLYWELL HALT** Passing the Halt on its way to Bolton Abbey is the trailer-led Autocar on its first trip following the Trailers' launch at the 2024 Transport Festival on 25 May.

HOLYWELL HALT During its loan spell at the E&BASR *Vulcan* also visited 'galas' at other heritage railways and returned to the Yorkshire Line facing Bolton Abbey. This gave opportunities for alternative photography locations such as here on the approach to the Halt from Embsay. *(7 May 2023)*

Right: As the train leaves Holywell Halt bound for Embsay, an old footbridge comes into view. This is another great vantage point for photography. *Karl Heath*

Below: On Christmas Eve 2022 the two train Santa Specials saw the Bolton Abbey facing *Beatrice* and Embsay facing *Cumbria* on the festive trains. In lovely winter light I was able to photograph both from the bridge within the space of 20 minutes.

The Embsay & Bolton Abbey Steam Railway

Left: **SKIBEDEN** J94 Class 68067 emerges from the shadows with a demonstration freight working during the railway's Transport Festival on 25 May 2024.

Below left: **SKIBEDEN** The 1903 NER Railcar and Trailer pass by on a lovely spring day.

Below: **SKIBEDEN** On the 8 September 2022, in the final light of the day, Andy Booth's Lancashire & Yorkshire Railway 'A' Class 52322 heads back to Embsay at the end of that day's photo charter.

Above: **SKIBEDEN** The area between the footbridge and Embsay is known as Skibeden and the line runs in the shadow of former quarry workings.

Right: **SKIBEDEN** In 2019 0-6-0ST *Jessie* spent the summer working services on the line. Built as Hunslet Works Number 1973 in 1937, it visited courtesy of the Pontypool and Blaenavon Railway. Here it is powering along the climb away from Embsay. *Will Smith*

SKIBEDEN 52322 heading to Bolton Abbey through the Dales landscape with the former quarry on the left, the expanding residential developments at Embsay in the centre and Embsay Crags to the right. *Karl Heath*

EMBSAY STATION

The Embsay & Bolton Abbey Steam Railway

The Embsay & Bolton Abbey Steam Railway

Left: **EMBSAY** Andy Booth's Lancashire & Yorkshire Railway 'A' Class 52322 arrives back at Embsay on 10 July 2022.

Below: **EMBSAY** The masked passengers and staff in this 29 September 2020 photograph are a reminder of the Covid-19 pandemic that swept the world at the beginning of that year. The railway had only reopened, after lockdown, two months earlier.

The Embsay & Bolton Abbey Steam Railway

2020 – The Coronavirus pandemic created distress and anxiety for everybody across the world to say nothing of the resultant financial chaos. The unprecedented late March lockdown restrictions that left towns and cities eerily deserted also had a massive impact on the heritage railway movement which saw all of Britain's standard and narrow gauge railways completely shut down virtually overnight.

Thankfully while the railway was put into a 'care and maintenance state' for what was to be a four-month period, behind the scenes the powers that be, with volunteer help, put together a workable and safe method for the operation of the railway once restrictions were lifted. So on Saturday 25 July these plans were put into place as *Illingworth* worked the first 'post-Covid' trains.

Below: **EMBSAY** *Illingworth* departs Bolton Abbey with the very first 'post-Covid' service.

The Embsay & Bolton Abbey Steam Railway

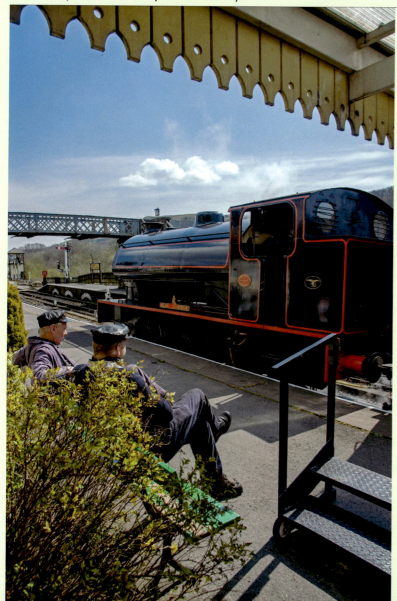

Scenes around the station in more tranquil times.

Right: **EMBSAY** Embsay station during the 1940s Weekend in 2020. A real vintage scene with the 1903 NER Railcar in platform 2 and many period dressed re-enactors milling around platform 1.

Below: **EMBSAY** 17 April 2021 was a Vintage Trains day with visiting 0-6-0ST *Welsh Guardsman* in charge of the Stately Trains six-wheelers.

77

Left: **EMBSAY** 10 July 2022 was a lovely summer's day for passengers on that days 'Dales Dining' service with Hunslet 0-6-0ST *Beatrice,* at the head of the train, about to depart Embsay.

Right: **EMBSAY** You can't get much more vintage than this scene from the 'Railway Rally' event in June 2021. Departing Embsay, built in 1888, with a vintage train of Victorian carriages was a double header comprising the 1890 built *Lucie* and 0-6-0 'Terrier' Class *Knowle* that dates from 1880. With the 1903 NER Autocar alongside platform 2 the combined ages of the locomotives, stock and buildings in view totals 927 years!

Most 'off peak' services terminate at Embsay. However in high season and at some special event weekends locomotives with trains from Bolton Abbey will pass through the station to run-round at Bow Bridge loop just before the former junction with the Grassington branch. On a bitterly cold December day back in 2017 0-6-0ST *Norman* was on Santa Train duties and is about to enter the run-round loop at Bow bridge.

The Embsay & Bolton Abbey Steam Railway

In this view over the village, Embsay Station is just out of sight to the right and the Grassington line can be see curving away to the left. *Karl Heath*

On the 1 January 1922 the Lancashire & Yorkshire Railway and London and North Western Railway amalgamated. 100 years later having, at that time, one Director's Saloon from each company in the Stately Trains Collection, the railway held a Centenary Weekend on 3/4 September, pairing the two Saloons behind the former Lancashire & Yorkshire Railway locomotive 52322. The Centenary Train seen here arriving at the loop.

In this 7 May 2023 view visiting *Vulcan* has run round its vintage train at Bow Bridge and is setting off back to Embsay ready to start the next journey along the stunning Embsay & Bolton Abbey Steam Railway.